China
a travel adventure

photography by Steve Vidler

text by Lorien Holland

PERIPLUS

Published by Periplus Editions with editorial office at 130 Joo Seng Road #06-01, Singapore 368357.

ISBN 0-7946-0319-X

Printed in Malaysia

Distributors

Asia Pacific Berkeley Books Pte Ltd
130 Joo Seng Road, #06-01/03, Singapore 368357
Tel: (65) 6280 1330; Fax (65) 6280 6290
Email: inquiries@periplus.com.sg
www.periplus.com

Indonesia PT Java Books Indonesia
Kawasan Industri Pulogadung
Jl. Rawa Gelam IV No. 9, Jakarta 13930
Tel: (021) 4682 1088; Fax: (021) 461 0207
Email: cs@javabooks.co.id

Japan Tuttle Publishing
Yaekari Building 3rd Floor, 5-4-12 Osaki
Shinagawa-ku, Tokyo 141 0032
Tel: (03) 5437 0171; Fax: (03) 5437 0755
Email: tuttle-sales@gol.com

North America, Latin America & Europe
Tuttle Publishing
364 Innovation Drive, North Clarendon
VT 05759-9436
Tel: 1 (802) 773 8930; Fax: 1 (802) 773 6993
Email: info@tuttlepublishing.com
www.tuttlepublishing.com

Front endpaper: The larger-than-life Terracotta Warriors guard the tomb of Qin Shihuang, the first emperor of a united China.

Page 1: Girls wearing the imperial dress of the Manchu Qing dynasty.

Page 2: A young boy poses in front of the Temple of Heaven in Beijing.

Right: The Forbidden City lies directly on the imperial line of power and was home to 24 Ming and Qing dynasty emperors. Its vast courtyards were only opened to visitors after the fall of the Qing dynasty in 1911.

Pages 6–7: The Great Wall near Beijing snakes away over the mountain peaks. In total the wall stretches 3,700 miles (6,000 kilometers).

Pages 8–9: The new financial district of booming Shanghai rises on the site of a former marsh.

Pages 10–11: A fisherman navigates the Li River near Guilin. His cormorants have rings around their necks so that they can catch fish for him but cannot eat the fish themselves.

Pages 12–13: Guangzhou's slick new airport opened for business in 2004, and remains the busiest airport in China.

Back endpaper: Shenzhen, one of China's newest cities, puts on a cultural performance that shows Beijing's ancient imperial might.

Exploring the Middle Kingdom

Images of China are nestled deep into most national psyches. From ancient Rome onwards, tales of the splendid riches and civilization of China have filtered through Asia and onto the West. Silk, tea and gunpowder all came from those mysterious lands of emperors and eunuchs. So did foot-binding and ideological upheaval. And of course, millions upon millions of people.

Now that China has opened her doors to foreign capital, and manufactured goods are flooding overseas in ever-increasing volumes, a new image is building. You are highly likely to be wearing a piece of clothing from China. Your mobile tele-phone, computer and DVD player could be from China, and you may well have spotted mainland Chinese tourists in your own town or city.

Still, the wholesale pumping out of modern goods and the growing numbers of Chinese making trips overseas does not mean that China has morphed away from its mystery and into a user-friendly shopping mall. Chinese arts, society, language and bureaucracy are still part of a civilization that is very, very different. Even for the ethnic Chinese of southeast Asia, who have only left their homeland for a few generations, China can seem like a foreign country.

Opposite: A tai chi devotee limbers up in the early morning light. He is practicing his movements beside the West Lake in Hangzhou, which is the most famed lake in China on account of its numerous arched bridges and pavilions, and the poems and paintings they have inspired.

Below: Morning exercise on the Bund in Shanghai, with the modern developments on the east side of the river in the background.

The Huangshan, or Yellow Mountain, range lies to the southwest of Shanghai and has been a place of pilgrimage for 1,200 years. It is linked to legends about the elixir of life, comprises 72 craggy peaks and has been the subject of countless poems and paintings.

My first images of China came from a small, musty book shop in London, where my parents bought me piles of slender little story books from the New China Press. That was back in the early seventies and the heyday of Communist propaganda, and I grew up reading about Chinese children who bravely fought through snow storms to rescue the commune's sheep or were fiercely loyal to their country whether they came from the temperate south or the frigid wilds of the north.

Still, I didn't understand the extent of China's isolation since the Communist Party took control in 1949, or appreciate its widescale poverty and backwardness. So my first visit to China in 1991 came as something of a shock.

I arrived on an overnight ferry boat from Hong Kong into the southern city of Guangzhou on a hazy autumn morning. Standing on the deck of the ferry, I still imagined I could spot a fresh-faced story-book revolutionary here or there, sitting on the back of her mother's bicycle, or squashed between adults on a packed public bus.

Then I cleared immigration and was through the bamboo curtain.

Gone was the reserve and disinterest of world-wise Hong Kongers. Gone were thoughts of my propaganda story books. I was right there, in the action. To be more precise I was fast becoming *the* action as people crowded round to get a look at the startled blonde girl standing on their quay.

Before long, a middle-aged immigration official shooed the crowd away, and found me a taxi. It was a big old-fashioned car, with a wide back seat upholstered in fraying deep red velveteen. Soothing music was playing on the radio and I sank gratefully into this oasis of calm.

Several months later I began studying Mandarin Chinese at the People's University in Beijing, and I learned that China itself has a great fear of chaos, of lack of order across its vast domains. As the country is about the size of Europe and stretches from bleak desert in the north, to great mountains in the west and lush rice paddies in the south, this is far from surprising.

Left: Chinese tourists pose for photographs in traditional costumes. Since the economic reforms of the nineties, there has been a resurgence of interest in China's past.

Below: Dancing partners practice their steps in a park in the western city of Chengdu, Sichuan province.

Right: Girls pose for photographs in imperial costumes.

中华人民共和国万岁

世界人民大团结万岁

Maintaining control and peace over China has been a preoccupation for many millennia.

China's two most influential philosophers, Laozi and Confucius, lived in the earlier part of the Chinese empire, when conflict between rival emperors was practically endemic. Both were naturally obsessed with order and calm, and avoiding chaos. Laozi, who was born around 604BC, laid out his ideas that people should live in peace and harmony with nature in a tome called the *Daodejing*, which became the philosophical basis of Daoism.

A generation later Confucius (551–479BC) began a more formulaic treatise on the duties and responsibilities of people, and in particular officials, called the *Analects*. His ideas only became well-known after his death, but they took a firm hold on the imperial system and became the basic training for government officials until 1911.

Confucian codes of conduct also became inextricably bound up in the fabric of Chinese society. This emphasis on tradition meant China was very slow to modernize and adjust herself to the rising power of Europe and later Japan.

After the collapse of the Qing dynasty in 1911, China fell into decades of chaos and conflict. Although many hoped Mao Zedong would restore order when the communists came to power in 1949, more upheaval followed, first in the Great Leap Forward (1958–60) and then the Cultural Revolution, which started in 1966.

Only after Mao's death in 1976 did China start to settle down and adjust to the modernity that had swept through other parts of the world. After slow initial progress, things changed dramatically in 1992 when China endorsed massive reforms that condoned private enterprise.

Massive economic expansion means cities like Shanghai have returned to the world stage. New buildings, new roads, new airports and new cities have sprung up like bamboo shoots. Cars have replaced the trusty bicycle as the main mode of transport in urban areas, and Chinese citizens are now permitted to travel overseas.

最高指示
你们要关心国家大事，要把
无产阶级文化大革命进行到底！

毛主席永远和我们心连心
——毛主席第七次檢阅文化革命大军

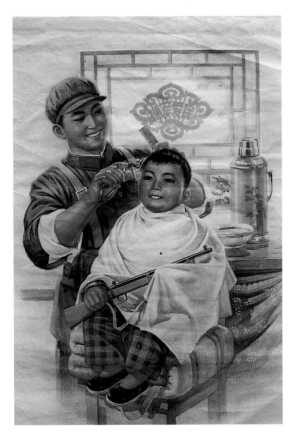

Top: A movie poster entitled "Chairman Mao's heart and our hearts are together." Produced during the Cultural Revolution, the movie documented Mao's seventh inspection of the revolutionary Red Guards.

Far left: The People's Liberation Army (PLA) played a major role in the formation of New China. To build feelings of loyalty to the army, there were several propaganda campaigns to publicize the devotion of the soldiers to the people.

Left: During the Cultural Revolution, China reinvented traditional performances to include class struggle themes. This poster depicts a ballet entitled "The Red Detachment of Women."

Opposite: Propaganda posters were honed to a fine art during the seventies. In "Looking Afar," published shortly after Mao Zedong's death, Mao strikes a father-like pose with a group of smiling children to symbolize his influence over the next generation of revolutionaries.

Such rapid reforms have come at a high price. While cities like Shanghai host the world's gliterati and Beijing prepares for the 2008 Olympics, many rural parts of China have fallen far behind the growth cycle and remain in desperate poverty. The environmental costs of such speedy growth are also high.

For the visitor, that means there is still plenty to excite the eye and frustrate the mind. And its not all in the present, for a continuity of sorts remains with China's lengthy past. Take the famed Huangshan or Yellow Mountains to the southwest of Shanghai, which have been a pilgrimage point for more than 1,200 years. Countless painters and poets have trudged around the craggy peaks seeking inspiration over the centuries. While the main route up is chaotically jammed with day trippers, you don't have to step far off the beaten track to find breathtaking views and a few moments of peace and harmony with nature. Laozi surely would have approved.

Top: Qingdao airport's new passenger terminal opened in May 2004. It was the most impressive of four new terminals that were opened that week across China. As China's economy grows at a hurtling pace, air travel has become increasingly common.

Left: As Shanghai increasingly assumes a role on the world stage, there is a growing sense of triumphalism in its architecture. The 87-floor Jinmao Tower is the fourth tallest building in the world, and the top half is the Grand Hyatt Shanghai. But its status as China's tallest building will soon be eclipsed by the World Finance Tower, planned for 101 storeys on a neighboring site.

Top: The Oriental Plaza in Beijing is on the Avenue of Eternal Peace, near Tiananmen Square. It replaced a block filled with communist-era shops and is home to many upscale western brand names.

Above: China's new economic strength has rekindled its love affair with food. In Shanghai's upscale Xintandi dining plaza, French, Cantonese, Thai, Italian, Sichuanese and Hunanese food is available.

Right: Shanghai is reestablishing itself as a fashion capital of the world, and has hosted most of the world's top designers in the last few years.

Although China is becoming increasingly wealthy, roadside stalls selling cheap food like fried noodles **(above)** and steamed wheatflour buns **(right)** remain very popular.

Top: Roasted ducks hang in a restaurant window in Shanghai.

Opposite: A meal of steamed dumplings laid out in a tourist restaurant in Shanghai.

Beijing: Emperors, Communists and Capitalists

Flying into Beijing on a clear summer day is a great way to get a grip on China's imperial capital. As the plane begins its descent, the arid Mongolian grass-lands to the north of the city give way to a craggy mountain range. Just as the mountain range gives way to the fertile Beijing plain, the watchtowers and garrisons of the snake-like Great Wall become visible on its southernmost peaks. Below them, the temple structures of the imperial Ming tombs appear, nestled among green fields. Within seconds, the northern edges of the city are in view, and then the approach lights of the runway.

Imagine for a moment that the plane didn't have to land but could continue flying south at this low altitude. After the airport, the fifth ring road would appear, an oblong highway that encircles the fast-expanding city. Shortly afterwards, the

fourth and third ring roads would come into view, and then the second ring road, which is built on the remains of the ramparts of ancient Beijing.

Next, you would glimpse the sparkling yellow roofs of the most important structure in China, the Forbidden City, home to 24 Ming and Qing emperors from 1421 to 1911. The imperial axis, which metaphorically channels all power and authority in China, runs due south through the Forbidden City and its majestic throne room to the center of it all—the Gate of Heavenly Peace, or Tiananmen.

The gate divides the Forbidden City from vast Tiananmen Square to the south, and is far more than a gate in the Western sense of the word. It is a large structure of vermillion red with an impressive marble balustrade, topped with a two-storey pavilion that can hold several thousand people.

Opposite: Chairman Mao memorabilia laid out for sale on a stall outside Mao Zedong's Mausoleum on Tiananmen Square. The building was constructed after Mao's death in 1976, and crowds still stream past his embalmed body on a daily basis.

Left: An elite guard standing at attention at the Gate of Heavenly Peace. Built in 1417, this rostrum is the symbolic center of power in China. Tiananmen Square lies to the south and the Forbidden City to the north, and a large portrait of Mao Zedong hangs over its central entrance.

It was here that the emperors appeared to their people and announced their decrees in front of kneeling dignitaries. It was also here that Mao Zedong declared the founding of the People's Republic of China in 1949. Although Chairman Mao died in 1976 and many of his policies have been reversed, his portrait still hangs over the main door, at the symbolic heart of China.

Tiananmen Square lies directly to the south of the gate, on a continuation of the imperial axis. It is reputedly the largest urban plaza in the world, with standing capacity for 600,000 people, and is where students gathered in 1989 to stage their pro-democracy demonstrations. Other significant demonstrations happened here in 1919 and 1976 as China moved through the turmoil of the fall of the Qing dynasty, republicanism, foreign occupation, civil war and the Cultural Revolution.

In the middle of the vast expanse of concrete sits Chairman Mao's mausoleum. Inside, Mao's body lies in a discreetly lit crystal coffin in front of an engraved homage which reads "Eternal praise be to Chairman Mao, our great leader and master."

Two top-heavy triumphs of Stalinist architecture flank the square itself—the Great Hall of the

Top: Chinese tourists queue up to view the embalmed body of Chairman Mao Zedong in Tiananmen Square. Mao, looking smaller and more frail than he appeared in life, lies in a crystal sarcophagus.

Above: Posing for a photograph in front of the Gate of Heavenly Peace is practically a patriotic duty for Chinese tourists. This eager young girl holds up two Chinese flags for good measure.

Right: The Gate of Heavenly Peace bedecked with rows of flowers ahead of National Day. Chairman Mao proclaimed the establishment of the People's Republic of China here on October 1, 1949.

Top: The Forbidden City was completed in 1421 and was the residence of 24 Ming and Qing emperors. The best of its collection of jades, bronzes and paintings was taken to Taiwan by retreating Nationalist forces in 1948, but there is still plenty to see in its various courtyards.

Above: The Gate of Supreme Harmony in the Forbidden City is flanked by a pair of fierce bronze lions, guardians of imperial might. This is the female of the pair as she has a cub playing under her left foot.

People to the east and the Museum of Chinese History to the west. Both were completed in 1959, just before the Sino-Soviet split, with sheer people power. Flush with revolutionary zeal, Beijingers toiled on the buildings after finishing their day jobs and got them completed in ten months.

The Chinese capital started life as a small frontier base, important mainly as a staging ground for campaigns against the nomadic peoples north of the mountains. In the 10th century these nomadic peoples pushed south and founded a walled city that eventually boasted a population close to one million. That in turn fell to the Mongols, and when the great Mongol leader Kublai Khan took control of all China in 1279, he made the city his capital.

Beijing's remarkably straight avenues, like the grand boulevard that runs below the Gate of Heavenly Peace, originate from this time, as do the small lanes that crisscross the grid—these are called *hutongs*, a corruption of the Mongolian word *hottog*, which means water well.

The Mongolians were also responsible for a grand irrigation scheme that guaranteed water to the city and created a series of pleasure lakes to

正大光明

Top: The splendidly decorated Imperial Throne in the rather vast and gloomy Hall of Supreme Harmony. This is where the emperor, or Son of Heaven, was crowned and married. He also commissioned high-ranking military officials and interviewed the top candidates in the imperial examinations from his throne.

Right: A ceiling detail from the imperial throne room, showing a magnificent golden dragon, the symbol of the emperor. The smaller round images depict the phoenix, symbol of the empress.

the north of the Forbidden City. The Italian traveler Marco Polo's descriptions of Beijing at this time are full of wonder at its splendors, which were unmatched in the Western world.

In contrast, modern Beijing is a seething mass of humanity and bureaucracy. As the capital city for most of the past 800 years, it houses all central government ministries, central military command and high-level delegations from each of China's provinces, regions and municipalities. It is also the center for state-sponsored art troupes, musicians and acrobats and boasts most of China's best universities, libraries and archives.

Sporadic attempts to control migration and rein in Beijing's explosive population growth have not met with much success. The government estimates a population of 15 million by 2008. That's a good nine million more than in 1949, and explains much of the faceless tower blocks that emanate from the city center. Beijing today is largely a proletarian sprawl, jammed with vehicles, prone to dust storms, and absolutely full of people.

But there are of course many pockets of imperial splendor, and quiet oases of calm just off many of the noisy grand avenues. One of the best

Left: A young girl, dressed in the auspicious color of red indulges in one of China's national pastimes—photography.

Above: Most of the thousands of visitors to the Forbidden City are domestic tourists. These two couples pose for a photograph in imperial garb—something that would not have been permitted in the days of the emperor.

Top: The Hall of Supreme Harmony, or throne room, is deeply symbolic. Its 24 pillars correspond to the hours of the day. Bronze crane and tortoise incense burners on the terrace symbolize longevity. A sundial and grain measure are symbols of imperial justice, and the marble dragon carved in the central steps is a symbol of the emperor.

Top: The defensive moat that surrounds the Forbidden City is 165 feet (50 meters) wide. The earth excavated to make the moat was so voluminous that it was piled up in a large hill to the north of the Forbidden City. The water freezes in winter and the moat is used for recreational skating.

Right: Tourists take a rest in a secluded courtyard in the Forbidden City. There are a mind-boggling 9,000 rooms in all the palaces and pavilions of the Forbidden City.

Top: Wangfujing is the most prestigious shopping street in Beijing. It was pedestrianized in the late nineties, and many old department stores were torn down to make way for massive shopping centers like the Xin Dong An plaza.

Right: Two decades ago, it was hard to find a bite to eat after nightfall in Beijing. Now late-night food markets abound. This stall sells kebabs of various meats and fish that are barbequed on demand.

Top: An old-style department store on Dazhalan, south of Tiananmen Square. The road retains much of its old architecture and is a heady mix of herbal medicine emporiums, silk shops, theaters and department stores specializing in clothes and furs. Several of the shops have entrances to the maze of underground air-raid tunnels that were built in Beijing after the Sino-Soviet split in the early 1960s.

Left: Peking, or Beijing, duck has been one of China's most celebrated dishes for centuries. The process is a slow one to master, with chefs taking five years to get the hang of the basic process and fifteen years to master their skills. The process is a long and involved one, from raising the force fed ducks on the outskirts of Beijing to braising their carcasses in a malt sugar blend and then hanging them in special ovens to roast.

Peking Opera is a mix of singing, dancing, acrobatics, mime and dancing. Performances can extend to several days, although modern shows tend to last only a few hours. Before the communists came to power in 1949, all roles were played by men, which resulted in female characters appearing exaggeratedly feminine. Peking Opera was popularized in the West by the actor Mei Lanfang, who played female roles and was said to have influenced Charlie Chaplin. Peking Opera is usually a series of excerpts from well-known stories, rather than a western-style opera full of conflicts that need resolving. It is one of the newer Chinese arts, dating back only as far as the end of the 18th century. The color of facial makeup is symbolic of the character. Red indicates courage and loyalty, black righteousness, purple wisdom and bravery and white cruelty. Metallic colors symbolize supernatural powers.

Left: China has the biggest mobile phone ownership worldwide, at close to 400 million subscribers. The mobile phone was one of the first trappings of modernity to be welcomed—partly because of the complex bureaucracy involved in getting a fixed line.

Above: Sleek boutiques now occupy prime real estate in downtown Beijing.

Top: The layout of Beijing's grand avenues dates from the days of Kublai Khan. This road is the main east-west axis through the city, and runs between the Gate of Heavenly Peace and Tiananmen Square.

Above: Beijing's Oriental Plaza claims to be Asia's largest shopping complex and cost $2 billion to build. The city-within-a-city in downtown Beijing has five themed malls and 11 high-rise towers and was at the center of a corruption scandal in the late nineties which brought down the municipal government.

Right: The trusty bicycle is slowly being eclipsed by the car as the transport of choice in Beijing. But bicycles are still a popular form of transportation due to the growing traffic congestion on Beijing's roads.

The Temple of Heaven is stunning in its simplicity and laden with symbolism. The emperors performed the major ceremonial rites of the year here, to pray for good harvests, to seek divine clearance and atone for the sins of the people.
The temples are round and their bases square because of ancient Chinese beliefs that heaven is round and the earth is square. In imperial times, the roof tiles were arranged in in three colors: The top tier was blue, symbolizing heaven, the middle tier was yellow, representing the emperor and the bottom tier was green, representing the people.

The variations of rhythm, beat and tonal quality in Chinese music are highly distinctive. Stringed instruments are called silks and range from two-stringed instruments like the Erhu (right) to three-stringed pear-shaped lutes (left) and multi-stringed zithers (above and far right). Playing the zither has historically been seen as a mark of good upbringing. It is one of the four arts, which also include calligraphy, painting and Chinese chess, which were required for entry into high society. Sophisticated musical instruments emerged early in China. By the time of the Han dynasty (206BC–220AD) the imperial court had already set up an office to gather ancient tunes and folk songs, and had several musical troupes.

Chinese acrobats have been performing for more than two millennia, and acrobatics was one of the few traditional art forms condoned by Mao Zedong. The best troupes perform in Beijing and Shanghai, with a remarkable repertoire of contortions, balancing and sheer strength.

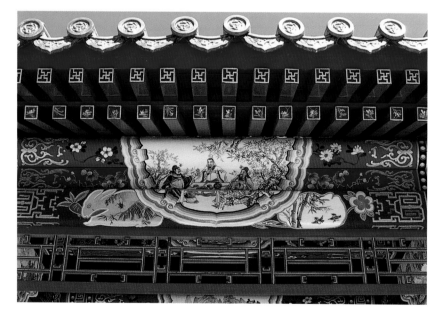

Top: The Qing emperors traveled to the Summer Palace by barge along imperial canals. The journey took two days. As they entered the southwest corner of the lake in the Summer Palace, they passed under the elegant Hunchback Bridge.

Above: A detail of the painted Long Corridor, which stretches nearly half a mile (700 meters), linking many buildings on the north shore of the Summer Palace lake.

Right and opposite: The Pagoda of Buddhist Virtue is the crowning glory of the Summer Palace and one of the tallest wooden buildings in China. The pagoda provides a charming view of the whole of the Summer Palace and suburban Beijing.

ways to get a feel for the pace and lifestyle of old Beijing is to duck into the *hutongs* that still exist in parts of the city center, particularly around the walls of the Forbidden City.

You will find crooked, tree-lined lanes, perhaps wide enough for two cars to pass in places. As you wind your way through, there will be little kiosks selling daily necessities, old grannies chatting and many enticing doors leading into courtyard houses. Some doors are restored to their former grandeur, indicating the presence of a rich or well-connected family. Others are piled high with bric-a-brac and coal briquettes for cooking and heating because the courtyard is subdivided to accommodate several families.

There are several courtyard gardens, far grander and more civilized than our little retreat, which are open to the public, particularly around the pleasure lakes north of the Forbidden City. The emperors themselves, especially during the final Qing dynasty, also took garden retreats very seriously. In the northern suburbs, close to the spring that supplied water to the imperial palace lie two such pleasure grounds. Both were built with large lakes, intertwining waterways, cleverly placed hills and numerous palaces and pavilions, and were the pride and joy of the imperial families. Both were also sacked and burnt by Anglo-French troops in 1860. The larger of the two, the Summer Palace, was rebuilt, and still stands today as a fine example of Chinese imperial architecture and the inspiration for many poets and artists.

Past the mountains on the north side of the Great Wall, and in a small town called Chengde lies an even larger imperial pleasure ground, built to escape the stultifying summers of Beijing, and known as "Fleeing-the-heat Mountain Villa." Villa is something of an understatement as the walls of the park are 6 miles (10 kilometers) long and the complex incorporates features from across the country, like a mini China assembled under the imperial gaze. Eight temples outside its walls celebrate China's might and her subjugation of the Tibetans, Mongols and other northern peoples.

Above: The stunning Badaling section of the Great Wall, which is one hour north of Beijing by road and was restored in 1957. The structure here runs across a mountain pass and defends the northern approach to the capital. In recognition of its key defensive role, the wall is wide enough to accommodate five horses or 10 men side-by-side.

Left: Entrepreneurial Chinese dress as an imperial guard (far left) and a Manchu princess (left) and earn a living by taking photos with tourists

But perhaps the most remarkable of the imperial pleasure palaces lies further north of Chengde, in the heart of the Mongolian grasslands. The 700-year-old earth embankments that once made up the walls of Yuan Shangdu, or Xanadu, are about a day's drive north from the capital, past the Summer Palace and the Great Wall and the "Fleeing-the-heat Mountain Villa."

Nothing remains today, save a large expanse of grassland and millions of pottery shards, but the poet Samuel Taylor Coleridge evokes the wonder of this original pleasure dome with some of the best-known lines in the English language:

> *In Xanadu did Kublai Khan*
> *A stately pleasure dome decree*
> *Where Alph the sacred river ran*
> *Through caverns measureless to man*
> *Down to a sunless sea.*

An apt beginning to the imperial Chinese legacy that ran through Kublai Khan and onto the Ming and Qing dynasties.

The Qing emperors con-
structed the "Fleeing-the-Heat
Mountain Villa" complex in
northern Chengde. It was built
like a modern-day theme park,
with references to most of
imperial China's important
gardens and temples. The
70-foot (22-meter) high
Buddha in the Temple of
Universal Tranquility (above)
has 42 arms and an eye in
each palm, and attracts thousands of tourists and worship-
pers each year.

The Temple of Universal Happiness **(top)** and the facsimile of Lhasa's Potala Palace **(above left and right)** are two of the eight remaining temples built by the Qing emperors in Chengde to hammer home the message of China's strength and unity. They marked the subjugation of the Tibetans, Mongols and other northern peoples.

出口
EXIT

入口
ENTRANCE

WELC

Shanghai: China's Mega Metropolis

Opposite: The Oriental Pearl TV Tower opened in 1994 in marshland across the Huangpu River, and heralded the start of Shanghai's rebirth. The curiously-shaped tower is now surrounded by skyscrapers, but still attracts hordes of tourists who ride elevators to the top to admire Shanghai's skyline.

Below: In a classic Shanghai blend of east and west, a street performer roller skates through a maze of soft drink bottles while performing a traditional Chinese fan dance.

Shanghai is China's phoenix, a world-class city rising from the ashes of its past. It is brash, glitzy, fast-paced, cosmopolitan and the absolute antithesis of staid Beijing. Those that love her glamor call her the Pearl of the Orient, and point to her current status as the global darling of both investors and glossy lifestyle magazines. To her detractors, she is the Whore of the East, a symbol of decadence, transience and China's past colonization and shame.

Still, that heady mixture makes for a good place to visit. Shanghai is the largest city in China, with a population of more than 20 million and some of the most visionary architecture in Asia. Its people are also some of the best self-publicists in the country. Back in 1993 when I first visited Shanghai, for a few damp and miserable days in early January, there was one phrase I heard over and over again—"New York, Paris, London and Shanghai." When I tentatively pointed out that the city was hardly in the same league as the world's big metropolises, out came the same reply—"Ah yes, but it will be. That is our rightful place."

Until the Communist Party came to power in 1949, Shanghai was indeed in the Big League, with the tallest buildings in Asia and more motorcars than the rest of China put together. The world's great trading houses flocked to build grandiose empire-like headquarters along the Bund. The soup of choice was borscht, brought by Russians fleeing the Bolsheviks, and the guards were Indian Sikhs, courtesy of the British Raj. There were adventurers, missionaries and foreigners from every corner of the globe seeking their fortunes alongside Chinese tycoons. The British alone had 400 million pounds sunk into the place and in 1935 Fortune magazine described Shanghai as the megalopolis of Asia and the "inheritor of 19th-century London and 20th-century Manhattan."

Under the glitz, there was also a nasty underbelly of exploitation and vice. Most workers lived in horrible slums, opium addicts numbered hundreds of thousands, and children were often sold into slavery and prostitution. In the concession areas—effectively colonized parts of China—parks

The Shanghai Grand Theatre (above and opposite) and the Shanghai Museum (left), both on the People's Square, are ambitious new additions to the city and evidence of its resurging arts and culture scene. The museum has a vast and well-displayed collection of 120,000 objects from China's past; many pieces survived because their owners hid them during the Cultural Revolution.

Opposite and below: The Bund is Shanghai's most photographed thoroughfare. Its neo-classical buildings are now home to some of the most exclusive restaurants in China, but the pedestrianized area near the river is still open to all, and is a popular place for locals.

Pages 62–63: The Nanpu Bridge is a symbol of the city's rapid economic development. When it opened in 1991 it was the first bridge linking Shanghai proper to the new Pudong financial zone. Now there are three other bridges over the Huangpu river.

sported signs that declared "No Dogs or Chinese Allowed." These fiery ingredients meant the city was always close to becoming a hot bed of unrest.

Indeed, the Chinese Communist Party held its first meeting in Shanghai in 1921. They gradually grew strong enough to organize significant labor strikes and in 1927, the Nationalist leader Chiang Kai-shek wiped out their Shanghai base to cement his hold on power. After that, the heady world of Shanghai just kept spinning, through the Japanese occupation and the end of World War II, until the Communists, who had regrouped into a rural movement under Mao Zedong, came to power and the defeated the Nationalists fled to Taiwan. When the Communist Party came to power in Beijing in 1949, the rich of Shanghai were still dancing. The city bowed out to communism in a rapacious whirl of pleasure, exploitation and squalor.

Much of Beijing's disdain for Shanghai stems from the latter's youth. Beijing, a capital city for close on 800 years, sees Shanghai as an upstart.

Before the British forced a concession port into the walled city of Shanghai in 1842, her population was a tiny 50,000 and her main industries were fishing and weaving. But by the fall of the Qing dynasty in 1911, Shanghai was parceled into several international settlements, was a major trading entrepot and saw itself in the front ranks of China's march into the modern age.

Towards the end of the 1960s, Shanghai was the powerbase of the Gang of Four, a group led by Mao's wife who led China into the disastrous Cultural Revolution. But after Mao's death, the city was kept firmly under Beijing's thumb. Only in the mid-nineties did President Jiang Zemin, a former mayor of Shanghai, grant his old domain the same economic freedoms as the rest of China.

Shanghai was of course raring to go. Many of those who had fled to Taiwan, Hong Kong, Europe and the United States returned, ready to invest funds and expertise. The marshland across the river became the futuristic Pudong financial district, with its gleaming skyscrapers and record-breaking bridges. A new road system, a new airport

Left : Nanjing Road is Shanghai's premier shopping street, and the stretch from the Peace Hotel on the Bund to the Park Hotel near the People's Square remains China's golden mile—although these days, it faces stiff competition from newer, swankier shopping malls.

Top: A panoramic view of the neo-classical architecture along the Bund. In the distance is the green-roofed Peace Hotel, formerly the Cathay Hotel. Like the Peninsula in Hong Kong, Raffles in Singapore, and the Taj in Bombay, this was the place to stay in Shanghai in the thirties.

Above: Shanghai attracts visitors from across China. These conference delegates are from southwestern Yunnan province.

Right: Young lovers taking a break on Shanghai's main shopping street, Nanjing Road.

Above: Almost a bird's eye view of the Huangpu river and the old city taken from the top of the Jin Mao Tower in new Pudong. In the foreground is the Oriental Pearl TV Tower.

Above right: "M" on the Bund is the grandfather of swank new restaurants on Shanghai's Bund.

Opposite: Plaza 66 is a swank 61-storey office tower and six-storey shopping emporium that was completed in 2000 in downtown Shanghai. It has a five-storey rooftop lantern that shines over the city.

and the fastest train in the world were put in. Between 1988 and 2002, the city redeveloped 20 percent of its residential space. It also put in a world-class museum on the People's Square.

Luckily, some of the old Chinese areas and some of the old colonial architecture of the foreign settlements, particularly in the French concession, survived the upgrade. Shanghai's most photographed thoroughfare, the Bund, emerged virtually unscathed. Bund is an Indian term imported with the British Raj. It aptly describes the embankment built on a muddy waterfront, but does not explain its grandeur or its mix-and-match assortment of edifices, built in neo-classical Manhattan style with a touch of old Europe.

The Bund now boasts some of the world's most expensive real estate, and has several establishments focusing on that ancient Chinese obsession with eating. Michelin-starred chefs rub shoulders with the best of China's regional cuisine. Prices and interior décor are definitely at the cutting edge, and evening views over the river into the shimmering Pudong financial district are stunning too.

The world's largest singe arch bridge stretches over the river into Pudong. And plans are afoot for the world's tallest building too—although several skyscrapers, including the Jin Mao Tower—already dominate the skyline.

Still, the older parts of Shanghai have no intention of allowing Pudong to take all the glory. The futuristically-named Tomorrow Square is a skyscraper redevelopment right in the heart of the city. Nearby is the ultra-modern Grand Theatre, the Shanghai Museum and the Shanghai Urban Planning Exhibition Hall, all clustered around a much-welcomed open space, the People's Square.

For a dose of the traditional side of Chinese culture, the heavily-visited Yu garden, at the edge of the old Chinese city, is replete with moon gates, bamboo clusters and weeping willows. But the best gardens of China are a few hours away by road in Suzhou, an ancient silk-making city on the route of the Imperial Grand Canal.

Chinese gardens are seen as works of high art—a fusion of architecture, nature and poetry. Cultured imperial officials often sought solace in personal kingdoms of tranquil pools, rockeries, bridges and pavilions. These had highly evocative names, such as the Palace of the Distant Fragrance and the Bridge of the Fleeing Rainbow. At its height in the Ming dynasty, Suzhou had more than 270 such gardens. Only a handful remain, but if you visit in the early morning or late afternoon, you can still experience the mood of calm contemplation that pervades the shaded pools and pavilions, and recharge your energy levels before returning to the frenetic activity of Shanghai.

The Xintiandi district (below) near People's Square is a rare example of Shanghai reclaiming its past rather than tearing it down. The five-acre (two-hectare) redevelopment of traditional two-storey tenement buildings is fast becoming a tourist attraction, with expensive bars, restaurants and cafes. New restaurants serve customers from across the world (bottom) although the traditional lion dance (right) is still the preferred way to open a new business.

Opposite: The Huxinting Tea House, at the entrance to the Yu Garden is a much visited, but still charming remnant of old Shanghai. The Yu Garden itself dates back to the 16th century.

Above: Shanghai's youth are as trendy and fashion-conscious as their counterparts in other major cities.

Left: Mahjong is a Chinese game, similar to the card game gin rummy. Gambling is often involved and the game was banned during the height of the communist era. Now it is popular once again.

Far left: Shanghai boasts many upscale boutiques from the world's leading luxury brands—and a whole industry of counterfeit goods. Copy-watch touts roam the major tourist sites in the city.

Top: Restaurant staff in down-town Shanghai perform their morning exercises before get-ting ready for the day's business.

Right: Ballroom dancing is a popular pastime across China. These couples are dancing on the Bund in central Shanghai.

Left: Street food is readily available in Shanghai. Steamed stuffed dumplings, or *baozi*, make a great mid-morning snack or simple lunch.

Below: Migrant workers from across China flock to Shanghai in search of work. This Muslim from the far northwest of the country is pulling noodles made from wheat flour for a traditional beef noodle soup.

Opposite: Food from every corner of China is available in Shanghai, as workers from all over the country pile into the city to work on construction sites and in private businesses. Eating on the move is also common on Shanghai's crowded streets.

Above: A clock repairer in the city of Shanghai makes minute adjustments to a timepiece.

Far left: Chinese silk was a wonder of the ancient world. For centuries, China prevented any outsiders finding out the secrets of production and even today it remains a major silk producer. Silk is readily available in Shanghai and other major cities in China.

Left: Dolls in the dress of China's minority population. There are 56 minority groups interspersed with the dominant Han Chinese.

Below left: Figurines dating from the Cultural Revolution in the late sixties. In the foreground are the "Gang of Four" who masterminded the entire campaign and beside them, kneeling, are intellectuals undergoing mass criticism.

Right: Calligraphy is a high art in China, and takes several years to master. Although there are only 11 basic brush strokes involved, these strokes may be combined to create over 40,000 characters.

Left: The Pagoda of the Northern Temple dates from the 17th century. The climb to the top is rewarded with superb views over the canals and gardens of Suzhou.

Right: Tourists feeding fish in the Grand Canal.

Far right: Monks visit the Pagoda of the Northern Temple. The nine-storey pagoda is 250 feet (76 meters) tall.

Below: The Master of the Nets Garden is one of the most picturesque of the Suzhou gardens. The New York Metropolitan Museum has a full-scale replica of its key pavilions.

Guangzhou and Shenzhen

Guangzhou was a key trading port when Beijing was little more than an imperial outpost, Europe was in the grip of the dark ages and Hong Kong was an unnoticed rocky outcrop. Almost two millennia later, it is still a key trading port, and commerce and trade run very deep in the city's psyche.

Even though southern Guangzhou is a long way from northern Beijing, it played a pivotal role in the opium wars with the British, in anti-imperial rebellions, and in nurturing Sun Yat-sen, the father of modern China. It also has its own flavor for the Cantonese tend to follow a great range of superstitions, be adventurous in their eating habits and speak a guttural language that is incomprehensible to speakers of Mandarin Chinese.

As the Cantonese have been exposed to international trade for several hundred years, they were also among the earliest groups of Chinese to emigrate. Today there are more than 20 million people living overseas in countries such as Singapore, Malaysia, South Africa, Australia and Canada who can trace their roots back to Guangzhou. With such a diaspora there are plenty of resources to plough back into the region.

The prolific Hong Kong film and music industry has also helped to create a strong and modern Cantonese culture. However, this doesn't always go down too well with the politburo in Beijing who perpetually worry about decentralization and a waning of their power.

Opposite: The modern skyline of Guangzhou is filled with skyscrapers, like the 48-storey Guangzhou International Trade Centre. This was built in 1996, four years after China kickstarted economic reforms in the south.

Below: Guangzhou city is cradled in a gracious bend in the Pearl River, and has been a regional trading center for many hundreds of years.

Guangzhou may be more famous as an economic powerhouse than a travel destination, but this doesn't mean it is a barren desert for travelers.

The Qingping market, deep in old Guangzhou, sells just about everything, from dried mushrooms, roots and herbs to cats, turtles and frogs. The Temple of the Six Banyan Trees, which was first constructed in 537 and still remains in active use, gives a feel for the age of the city. Shamian Island, a former British and French concession along the banks of the Pearl River retains some of its old world charm. The lively shopping areas on Xiajiu and Shangjiu roads sell clothes, trinkets and household goods—although they have nothing like the range of goods made in the thousands of factories in the region and exported through Guangzhou.

Despite its age, the overwhelming impression of the city is of skyscrapers, shopping malls, traffic jams and noise as its 10 million inhabitants compete for space. Much of the city's economic success has come in the last decade and is due to its location at the head of the Pearl River Delta. The Pearl River flows into the South China Sea past the special economic zones of Shenzhen and Zhuhai and the former colonies of Hong Kong and Macau.

For most of Guangzhou's history, these downstream locations were little more than sideshows to its own importance. But that has all changed. Hong Kong is a world-class cosmopolitan city and Shenzhen, the first of China's Special Economic Zones, has morphed from a fishing village into a city of eight million in 25 years. Filled initially with factories, and now with skyscrapers and shopping centers, the city has clocked up an average annual growth rate of more than 25 percent.

Most of the factories in Shenzhen churn out clothes, shoes and toys for overseas markets. Although nearly all of the workers are internal migrants, from the poorer western provinces, the city has the highest per capita income in China. It is also building parks and tourist facilities to attract more visitors from Hong Kong, which is a short train ride away. One of the most famous is Splendid China, which miniaturizes 84 major highlights of China into a 74-acre (30-hectare) park. Most attractions have been reproduced at a scale of 1:15, making it possible to visit the Great Wall, the Terracotta Warriors, the Forbidden City and the Three Gorges in an afternoon. Not quite the China travel adventure you will find in this book, but a start at least!

Opposite: Runners pass the 80-storey CITIC Plaza, the tallest building in Guangzhou. It was the tallest building in China when it was completed in 1997, but was eclipsed by the Jin Mao Tower in Shanghai in 1999.

Top: Bustling Xiajiu street is a great place to find a bargain item of clothing.

Right: Western-style wedding portraits complete with flowing white dresses and tuxedos are fashionable in modern Guangzhou. Most couples will also take a set of photographs in a traditional Chinese wedding outfit too.

Those who love
deeply cannot age.

Left: The five-storey Zhenhai Tower is the only part of Guangzhou's original city wall that still stands. Its foundations date back to 1380 and it was used as a watchtower to guard against pirate attacks. It is now a history museum and the cannons date from the opium wars, when British and French troops occupied the building.

Right: Sun Yat-sen, the father of modern China, was born near Guangzhou and made the city his powerbase. His memorial hall was built with private donations after his death from cancer in 1925 and remains an important building, partly on account of its traditional-style architecture and partly because it has space for 4,000 people.

Above and right: Xiajiu street in downtown Guangzhou is a pedestrian zone and its bright neon signs never fail to attract the evening shopping crowds.

Left: Qingping market is a crowded mass of stalls and shops that specialize in weird and sometimes wonderful things to eat, from dried mushrooms, roots, herbs and spices to live animals.

Top: Tourists in Shenzhen's Splendid China park pose for a photograph outside a miniaturized version of Beijing's Forbidden City, which is reproduced at a scale of 1:15.

Above: Roller skaters hone their skills outside the futuristic Shenzhen Civic Centre.

Right: An artist paints flowers onto a model for a sales promotion in a Shenzhen department store.

Right: A Shenzhen hotel door-man helps passengers out of their taxi. The 69-storey Shun Hing Square, Shenzhen's tallest skyscraper, is in the background.

Xian and the Yangtze River

Opposite: The Big Goose Pagoda is one of the few remaining buildings in Xian from the golden age of the Tang dynasty. It was built to house Sanskrit Buddhist scriptures from India and was originally constructed of rammed earth to make it fireproof.

Below: The Terracotta Warriors are Xian's main attraction. These date back to 210BC, but were forgotten until 1974 when some farmers digging a well uncovered the major archaeological find.

Once upon a time, Xian stood at the very center of the Chinese empire, and was probably the largest, most cosmopolitan city in the world. It was the starting point for the Silk Road trading routes to Central Asia, Russia, India, the Mediterranean and even Africa. Culture, architecture and literature reached new heights during this halcyon period and Arab Muslims, Persian Zorastrians and Syrian Christians all built places of worship in the city, alongside a forest of Buddhist temples.

When the golden age of the Tang dynasty ended in 907AD, power gradually moved east towards Beijing. Today's Xian bears little resemblance to its former self. Gone is the cosmopolitan melting pot, gone are the centers of power and the imperial splendor. Foreign residents now number only a few thousand, and modern factory emissions and coal burning appear to have made air pollution endemic.

When I arrived at the city's main railway station in late 2004, I felt I had traveled back in time by a decade. Fashions were out-of-date, bicycles still mattered, and most of the people around the station had not seen a foreigner at close quarters. Of course, that makes Xian all the more appealing for travelers. There is still plenty to see under the grime, as western China has not experienced the great economic boom of the east and Xian's old city is somewhat unscathed.

Xian's current city walls date from the 14th century and have a shorter perimeter than the Tang dynasty originals. The two surviving religious buildings from the Tang period—the Big Goose Pagoda and the Little Goose Pagoda—are south of the current ramparts. The fortress-like Big Goose Pagoda was built in 652AD to protect hundreds of tomes of Buddhist scriptures brought from India by the traveling monk Xuanzheng. The

The main underground vault of terracotta soldiers contains 6,000 larger-than-life sized warriors and soldiers in battle formation, primed to guard the tomb of China's first emperor. The figures in the foreground have been restored, while the back of the vault remains as it was when first discovered. Although the figures were originally painted, few traces of color now remain.

Little Goose Pagoda, built 50 years later for the same purpose, is a more delicate rendering.

Back inside the city walls, the great Bell Tower sits in the center of a modern roundabout, accessible only by an underpass. The tower dates back to the 14th century and used to contain a large iron bell that marked time. Now it is more useful as a marker for exploring the city. The area to the west of the tower is the city's old Muslim quarter, which is riddled with narrow lanes lined with market stalls, antique shops and food sellers. Muslim women wearing headscarves and men wearing white skull caps are easy to spot around the Great Mosque, which is one of the largest in China, and worth a visit because of its remarkable fusion of Islamic and Chinese architectural styles.

Xian's major site is the Terracotta Warriors, which lies outside the city in a series of buried vaults. They date back to 210BC and the death of Qin Shihuang, the first emperor of a unified China. When he had consolidated his power, he set up his capital near modern-day Xian and ruled with an iron fist. His tomb was fittingly grand, and included an army of larger-than-life-sized terracotta soldiers to stand guard over him.

China fell into chaos after the emperor's death, and the terracotta soldiers were forgotten until 1974 when farmers digging a well uncovered the major archaeological find. Some 7,000 figures and horses have so far been unearthed, and there could be more. The warriors are on the UNESCO list of world heritage sites, and are the second Chinese listing after the Forbidden City in Beijing.

Left: The fortress-like Big Goose Pagoda was originally a five-storey earth structure that collapsed in the 8th century. A brick tower offering great views of the city was built in its place.

Above: Antique and curio shoppers in the Beilin market, just inside the south gate of Xian's city walls.

Top: The 16th century Bell Tower is a dominant feature of central Xian, and its bell was rung each morning at dawn. It is located in the middle of a roundabout and can be accessed through an underground tunnel.

Above and right: Actors dressed in imperial costumes recreate the splendors of ancient Xian. Cultural performances such as these are a popular tourist draw.

Guangxi and Yunnan

Pages 94–95: The Reed Flute Cave in Guilin is a sea of stalagmites and stalactites. Its largest grotto, called the Crystal Palace of the Dragon King can hold 1,000 people and was used as a shelter from Japanese air raids during World War II.

Opposite: Laid back Yangshuo town lies on the Li River near Guilin and is a perfect place to contemplate the amazing limestone mountains that rise out of its lush paddy fields.

Below: Traditional fishermen on the Li River use cormorants to help them catch fish.

Picture-perfect scenery links southwestern Guangxi and Yunnan with the mighty Yangtze River. All three offer up the images of China you will have seen in postcards, books, and on chocolate boxes: The soaring peaks that rise out of lush paddy fields, the cobbled medieval streets bathed in early morning sunshine, the pretty towns nestled below snow-covered mountains and the narrow river gorges lined with high, rugged cliffs.

The most famous of all of China's picturesque spots is Guilin, in Guangxi Province, which is widely known as "the best spot under heaven." Guilin is an ancient city that first came to prominence during the building of the Lingqu Imperial Canal in 214BC. Here, narrow mountains rise one by one from the flat banks of the silk-like Li River. Boat trips down the waterway pass bucolic scenes of farmers guiding their buffaloes through paddy fields and fishermen and their cormorants collecting their catch on bamboo rafts.

Several hours down the river is the leisurely little town of Yangshuo, a welcome respite from busy Guilin. The scenery here is picture-perfect too and the narrow streets, with their legendary backpacker cafes serving muesli and banana pancakes, are a great place to while away the hours.

Small towns like Dali and Lijiang in Yunnan province are nestled below snow-covered mountains and offer up equally delightful cafes from which to admire the scenery.

Yunnan has an added advantage for the weary China traveler of having a remarkable blend of minority and tribal peoples, including the Yi, the Tibetans, the Bai and the Naxi.

Dali itself is in a Bai area, and was the center of two kingdoms (one of which stretched as far as Laos) until Genghis Khan conquered the region in the 13th century. A 16-storey pagoda dating from the 9th century still stands, flanked by two smaller towers. There are other ruins of Dali's past to see, but its hard to beat an afternoon of sitting still and admiring the Cangshan Mountains towering over the east of the town and the long finger-like Erhai lake sparkling to its west.

The narrow peaks jutting out of lush paddy fields near Guilin (left) are the best known scenery in China. The 8th century poet Han Fu described the mountains (below) as "kingfisher jade hairpins" rising out of a belt of fine green silk. Although tourist boats crowd the river during peak season, there is still enough space for traditional fishermen (right) to ply their trade.

Several hours' drive north of Dali is Lijiang. The old town is a charming maze of cobbled streets crisscrossed by canals and peppered with backpacker cafes.

To the north of Lijiang is the Black Dragon Pool park, with its Moon Embracing Pavilion. The backdrop is the stunning Jade Dragon Mountain range, which soars to 18,000 feet (5,500 meters). The far side of the range drops into the upper reaches of the Yangtze River, helping to form a series of magnificent, deep gorges. The deepest of these is the Tiger Leaping Gorge, where the Yangtze surges eastwards, some 12,800 feet (3,900 meters) below the mountaintops.

The Yangtze is China's longest river. It rises on the Tibetan plateau and makes its first large turn near Lijiang. It flows east across China to the sea near Shanghai, its course neatly dividing China into north and south, with winter-time heating only officially allowed to the north of the Yangtze.

Scenically, the most beautiful stretch is not in the Tiger Leaping Gorge, but in the Three Gorges, several hundred miles to the east between Chongqing and Wuhan. The river falls 500 feet (150 meters) as it passes through these narrow gorges, and at a number of spots there is a tricky mixture of raging torrents and dangerous shal-lows. Until 1898, when a series of blasting operations removed several hidden rocks and deepened the worst of the shallows, the gorges were only navigable by small boats. Now a two-day boat journey through the mountain peaks and rugged crags, it is one of China's major tourist attractions.

Downstream, the $24 billion Three Gorges dam is nearing completion. The dam is nearly one and a quarter miles (two kilometers) wide and will generate hydro-electric power and prevent flooding. The Yangtze has a huge variance in low and high water levels and breaches its banks almost every year, causing great devastation and loss of life. China has attracted a great deal of criticism over the environmental and social costs of such a grand scheme, but insists the benefits are sufficient to plough ahead.

The dam will raise water levels in the Three Gorges by around 10 meters, but that won't make much difference to the soaring cliffs. For those who like the Chinese preoccupation with seeing shapes and animals in rocks, there are countless features with whimsical names like the Valley of the Golden Helmet and Shining Armour and the Gathered Immortals Peak. Alternatively, you could just sit back, enjoy the view and write a few postcards as you float ever eastwards.

Left: The Naxi people are descended from Tibetan nomads and live mainly in and around the town of Lijiang, in the foothills of the Tibetan plateau. Their society was matriarchal until recent times, and the women still seem to run the show.

Above: A woman poses for tourists in her ethnic clothes.

Yunnan has nearly 30 different ethnic groups, including the Lisu hill tribes **(far left)** who live along China's border with Myanmar, and the Bai people **(left)**, who live in and around the ancient city of Dali.

Left: The Black Dragon Pool and the Moon Embracing Pavilion in Lijiang. Although the pavilion is constructed in Ming dynasty style, it had to be rebuilt in 1950 after a high ranking official and his lover set themselves on fire in a double suicide that also consumed the pavilion.

Right: Three pagodas dating from the 9th century dominate the skyline in Dali, and are reminders of the city's past importance as the capital of a kingdom that spread as far as Laos and northern Thailand.

Below: Five women pose in traditional Bai costume. The Bai ethnic group are centered around the ancient city of Dali.

Chinese poets and artists have long celebrated the rugged landscape and stunning beauty of Guilin. Today it is one of China's leading attractions, drawing thousands of tourists every year.

Further Adventures

China is littered with adventures just waiting to happen. Like traveling to the desert fort that marks the end of the Great Wall, or scrambling into caves to view ancient Buddhist carvings, or searching for pandas in the wilds of western Sichuan.

The panda is native to China and has long been regarded as a bringer of good luck and a great brand name for Chinese products.

But illegal hunting and economic development have pushed the species towards extinction, and only around 1,000 pandas are still living in the wild. The Woolong Nature Reserve in the wilds of Sichuan offers up the best chance to see a panda in its natural habitat. Plan to stay in the reserve for several days and hike out into the hills if you are dead set on seeing one, as the bamboo-eating panda is notoriously shy.

An adventure with a more certain outcome is a dip into China's ancient Buddhist cave carvings, which are rather easier to locate. The fine art of Buddhist cave sculpture originated in India and reached a peak in China in the 7th and 8th centuries. When the Tang dynasty started to decline and abandoned its open-door policies, foreign religions such as Buddhism became subject to widespread persecution. Even though Buddhism recovered and eventually came to be seen as a Chinese religion, cave sculptures never regained their former prominence.

Some of China's most accessible cave sculptures are in central Luoyang, the capital of the Northern Wei Dynasty in the 5th and 6th centuries. The Northern Wei actively supported Buddhism and started to carve out a religious site on the slopes of the Dragon's Gate, or Longmen, mountains near the city. At its peak, there were 1,300 grottoes, 40 pagodas and close on 100,000 statues along the slope. But much has been damaged by natural erosion and early Western souvenir hunters who hacked off as much as they could cart away.

The cave sculptures near Datong, now a grimy coal city northwest of Beijing, were the precursors to the Longmen Grottoes. Although a smaller complex, the sculptures have suffered less damage, so foreign influences, such as Greek tridents and images of Indian Hindu gods are still visible.

Still, both complexes pale in comparison to the oldest and most impressive cave-temple complex, which is on the Silk Route in the far northwest region of China near the town of Dunhuang.

These caves were carved out of a sandstone cliff near Dunhuang over a 600-year period from 366 AD. As the caves grew larger, they were filled with wall paintings and stucco figures. Over time, interest and knowledge of the site waned, Islam became a competing religion in the area and Tibetan tribes people threatened to invade. So in the 11th century, the remaining monks filled one cave with about 60,000 Chinese, Tibetan, Sanskrit and Uighur documents and statues from the complex. Then they closed up the cave and dispersed.

Only in 1900 did a Chinese monk discover the sealed cave. A British explorer persuaded the monk to part with 29 packing cases of manuscripts,

Opposite: The 55-foot (17-meter) tall Vairocana Buddha was carved out of the Longmen mountains near Luoyang in the 7th century. The Buddha and disciples were originally sheltered inside a large cave, but the roof has since fallen in and the figures are now exposed to the elements.

Below: The panda is native to China, and is the nation's favorite mascot. However, its numbers in the wild are falling fast because of poaching and economic development. Panda diplomacy, via zoo exchanges with other countries, was also key in China's reintegration with the world after years of communist isolation.

paintings and art relics. Then a French traveler bought more of the manuscripts and was followed by American, Russian and Japanese collectors. At that point, imperial Beijing got wind of the discovery and the foreign intrusions and took the rest of the manuscripts back to the Chinese capital. That means no documents remain at Dunhuang, but the 492 caves that survived the ravages of time contain a wealth of statues and murals detailing Buddhist characters, episodes from the Sutras, legends and every-day scenes.

Jiayuguan Fort is the official western end of the Great Wall, and traditionally the last major stronghold of the Chinese empire. Today it is well within Chinese territory, and seven hours' drive towards the east from Dunhuang. But it is still an impressive construction, hunkered down in the arid wastes of western China to control a key pass that lies between snow-capped mountains.

The fort is about 3,700 miles (6,000 kilometers) from the other end, where the Great Wall meets the sea. It was built in 1372 shortly after the Ming emperors had forced the previous Yuan dynasty back onto their Mongolian steppe homelands north of the Great Wall.

The Ming dynasty paid great attention the rebuilding and defending the Great Wall but were eventually defeated by another set of northern nomads who broke through and went on to found the Qing dynasty. The Qing too were defeated in 1911, but the Great Wall remains—a testimony to the harsh realities of riding the Chinese tiger and a great place for a China adventure.

Above: Visitors clamber down sand dunes to the compound around the Crescent Moon Lake near Dunhuang. The lake is a geographical oddity because competing wind streams mean it never fills up with sand. However, over-development has already caused the lake to shrink to half its original size.

Right: Travelers take a camel train through the Singing Sand Mountains, south of the Dunhuang oasis. The mountains are so called because their sand is very fine and makes a singing sound as people run across it.

Top and above: The Jiayuguan Fort is the official end of the Great Wall. It was the last major stronghold of the empire, and the far western end of a 3,700-mile (6,000-kilometer) wall that starts at the Yellow Sea north of Beijing and snakes right across China.

Right: A sample of a Buddhist-themed painting from the Dunhuang cave complex. The cave's arid conditions mean the centuries-old pigments of azurite blue and cinnabar vermillion used in the paintings are still bright.

Opposite: The Dunhuang cave complex contains thousands of wall and ceiling paintings depicting Buddhist themes.

Page 112: The Terracotta Warriors were discovered in 1974, 23 miles (37 kilometers) east of Xian.